Guelp

819.154 PRIE
Priest, Robert
Reading the bible backwards /

MAR - 2009

READING THE BIBLE
BACKWARDS

Robert Priest

READING THE BIBLE
BACKWARDS

ECW PRESS

MISFIT

Copyright © Robert Priest, 2008

Published by ECW Press, 2120 Queen Street East, Suite 200,
Toronto, Ontario, Canada M4E 1E2
416.694.3348 / info@ecwpress.com

All rights reserved. No part of this publication may be reproduced, stored in a retrieval
system, or transmitted in any form by any process — electronic, mechanical,
photocopying, recording, or otherwise — without the prior written permission
of the copyright owners and ECW Press.

LIBRARY AND ARCHIVES CANADA CATALOGUING IN PUBLICATION

Priest, Robert, 1951–
Reading the Bible backwards / Robert Priest.

819,154
PRIES

Poems

ISBN 978-1-55022-835-9

1. Title.

PS8581.R47R42 2008   C811'.54   C2008-902427-3

Editor for the press: Michael Holmes / a misFit book
Type: Rachel Ironstone
Cover Design: David Gee
Author photo: Henry King
Printing: Coach House Printing

This book is set in Bembo and Century Expanded.

The publication of *Reading the Bible Backwards* has been generously supported by the
Canada Council for the Arts, which last year invested $20.1 million in writing and
publishing throughout Canada, by the Ontario Arts Council, by the OMDC Book Fund,
an initiative of the Ontario Media Development Corporation, and by the Government of
Canada through the Book Publishing Industry Development Program (BPIDP).

Canada Council   Conseil des Arts
for the Arts   du Canada

Canada

ONTARIO ARTS COUNCIL
CONSEIL DES ARTS DE L'ONTARIO

PRINTED AND BOUND IN CANADA

ECW PRESS
ecwpress.com

MISFIT

CONTENTS

3 3281 01346 516 3

ACKNOWLEDGEMENTS

My thanks to:

Huck Kirzner, Marsha Kirzner, Mildred Kirzner, Ted and Betty
Priest, Eli, Dan and Ananda, Allen Booth, Max Layton, Lance
Strate, and Michael Holmes.

Special thanks to Alannah Myles, who got me started on
this book.

This book remembers Irving Layton, Gilda Mekler, Eric Layman,
Bronwyn Dixon, Geri Tanner, and George "Otto" Carlin.

I would also like to express my gratitude to the taxpayers of
Canada, Ontario, and Toronto via their Arts Councils — The
Canada Council, The Ontario Arts Council and The Toronto Arts
Council — for their generous assistance on and off throughout
30 years of writing poetry.

Robert Priest's website is: www.poempainter.com

Dedicated to my true love, Marsha Kirzner

"The river flowed both ways. The current moved from north to south, but the wind usually came from the south, rippling the bronze green water in the opposite direction."
　— Margaret Laurence

"How will your tool reverse on you when it's pushed to its outer limit?"
　— Marshall McLuhan

"Life can only be understood backwards; but it must be lived forwards."
　— Søren Kierkegaard

"I buried Paul."
　— John Lennon

THE CODE

Coded into one language
Is the other language

Everything we say
We say something else

READING THE BIBLE BACKWARDS

Reading the bible backwards
Christ Jesus pops his nails
And comes down
To give the karma back to the people
Bearing the cross downhill
He shrugs off the scourging
Of his torturers
He escapes unscathed
From his backwards trial
Returned by Rome
To the Judas kiss

Reading the bible backwards
Christ Jesus says
Cursed are the meek
For the rich shall inherit the earth
He says turn the other cheek
Or I'll turn it for you
The moneychangers
Throw backwards Jesus
Out of the temple
And he wanders around
Giving people leprosy
And causing blindness
Reading the bible backwards
Christ Jesus turns the adulteress
Over to her judges
He puts the resurrected
Back to death
But they rise again
Like bread

After that he leaves
The living living
And the dying dying
He moonwalks rapidly
Out of history
Back to Mary's arms
In reverse birth
He shrinks
Through her womb
Rewound
To the infertile egg
And beyond

For a while there is a star
That hovers
Then that too is gone ·

ROUGH TRANSITIONS
FROM *DEITY* TO *THEORY*

deity *deity deity*
deeidee dee-uh-dee
dee aw-dee
tee aw-dee
thee aw-dee
thee-ah ee
theeyah-ee
theuh ee thee aw ree
theory theory theory
thee yaw ree
thee yaw ee
thee ah ee
thee uh ee
thee uh dee
theeuh tee
theity
teity
deity deity deity

FAITH IS TO WALK BACKWARDS

Faith is to walk backwards
Over pitfalls and rubble
Never looking behind
Faith is to face the future
And stride into the past

Great and holy are those
Who trek in reverse
Undoing doom after doom
Faith is to fall
Into the arms of maybe no-one
Faith is to trust
The ground will still be
At your heels

Moses led his people backwards
Through the desert
All the way to Egypt
Backwardness
Delivered Jonah
Breech birth
From the whale
It brought Eve to Adam
And Adam to Eden

It is a miracle when anyone walks backwards
A great distance
But Yeshua, the man who takes apart furniture
Is the only one to have walked backwards
On water

FACE/FAITH MEME SPLICE

To look at your faith in the mirror
Wanting to hide your faith
The faith behind your faith
A faith to die for
Just another pretty faith
The new faith of child poverty
It must be faithed
To fall flat on your faith
Faith it
A bald-faith liar!
So in your faith
Get out of my faith
You can't faith the truth
Utterly two-faithed
Faith to faith meetings
The faith that launched a thousand ships
The faithless masses
Just keep a smile
On your faith
A very unattractive
Faith
It's written all over
Your faith
I love you
For your faith
I dream of your faith
I can't get your faith
Out of my mind
I want to kiss your faith
I want to hold my faith
To yours
And see the tenderness

In your faith
To look into the very faith
Of god

THE LORD'S PRAYER BACKWARDS

Our father who art on earth
Dreadful be your name
May your kingdom never come
May your will be left undone
Here as it is in hell
You take from our mouths
The bread of every day
And hold our wrongs
Forever against us
As we hold ours
Against all
You lead us directly to damnation
And deliver us to the devil
For yours is the chaos
The weakness and shame
For never and never
A woman

IN THE BACKWARDS CHURCH

There is only one true backwards church
Born to carry on god's curse

Face to the wall its wheels squeal
Stuck in reverse

Its spiritual leader is always wrong
Everything he and all his predecessors

Ever said is incorrect
In the backwards church

Priests come between
You and god

They must be registered
Sex offenders

The screaming of children
Is everyone's favourite hymn

In the backwards church

They clang the bones of the dead
And read from pornographic texts

God prays to the people
But they don't listen

ANGLE/ANGEL MEME SPLICE

Diagonal angels
Haunting the periphery
Obtuse angels
Flat line angels
With no disappearing point
Angels are measures quanta
You have to consider every angel
All the angels of the room
And the angels of hats
All the angels in text books
The angels of firearms
And wrists hanging
At weird angels
What is the angel of intersection
The angel of the telescope
Who can calculate the angel of trajectory
Camera angels
Every angel has
An inverted other complementary angel
Between any two angels
There are infinite other angels
Every square has four right angels
She knew all the angels
She covered all the angels
The angel of the dangle
The angel of entry
The sum of two angels
Opening at an ever-increasing angel
Tilted at an unholy angel
Just what is her angel

There is no bad angel
Of her face
The view from any angel
Is divine

HERE IN BACKWARDS LAND

here in backwards land
the sun comes up at night
the blues plays us
but only at the other end
of the trumpet

we have laws
but they are expressly for breaking
our slogan is
gentleness by force
we fly our planes backwards
into perpendicular airstrips
then we sign a peace treaty
and the war starts

the pain is the same both ways
pain is not reversible
in your world
or ours

in our world
we make dust
and dust makes
god
hands first

we pray but
it is to ourselves

it is true we are a backwards people
we speak all the time
but only to subvert meaning

in both worlds
the truth is not reversible
it runs both ways
in my world we call it
the big lie

and we don't believe it
it is not logical
that birds can fly
water ought to be very dry
we go to get disease
from doctors
and sin from priests

we like to feast
on hunger though hunger is our dish
everything we do
we do to maximize
the pain

in our constitution it says
no one is equal
before the law
our first commandment is
thou shalt kill

we get to vote
but the winner is the loser

when we love one another
that's the worst

we break off all contact
we distance ourselves
we don't want anything
especially tenderness

we are driven by how much
we need to utterly avoid
having sex

we have evolved
to be repellent to one another

it is a disaster if we meet

if we mate in my world
that is tragedy
why reproduce? we ask
whenever a child is born

ARSE BOOK

Come look me in the eye
On arse book
I'll show you my naked
Other self
My cyclopean gaze
Full on

)*(

If you like the pants down glance
The vertical brow
If you like a wink at 90 degrees
Come and take in
This sideways leer
From the bottom of my soul
Dig these pix of my puckered pie-hole

)*(

Dark star eye bent
From many angles
My most earthen part
A kind of telescope
Whose pearl of backwards hope
Lays bare my secret heart
Tight between two clamshells
Pulled wide apart

)*(

SOUL/SOLE MEME SPLICE

Poor blind soles
How they are pierced
By the nail of the world
How they are bound and made numb
How the coldness of stone
Drains them
Flat out on the material plane
Unseen
Under appreciated
Yet they are first into the pit and last out
They are the provenance of all orgasm
It is our soles which bear us
Through the air uplifted
When we jump for joy

Our soles hide at the bottom of us
But they long to be stripped bare
And exposed
They want to upend gravity
And show their naked faces to the sky
O who can understand the delicate delving in our soles
The ancient scripts and intersects
Which make of each a map a riddle
No-one ever solves
Some say our soles are illusory
But to anyone with faith in their own senses
They are palpable
As certain as palms
They ground and balance us
They bear the weight of the body
And all the body bears too

Soles love a good groove
Sometimes with yoga
Two soles can hook into one another
Connect almost seamlessly
Mutual mirror images
They despair to think they are forever separated
Alone inside themselves
Never quite believing
Somewhere above
They meet in one cross-legged body
One mind

PUTTING UP BABEL

Putting up Babel
Time after time
We don't stop
And if someone
Unifies the language
We go dialectic, megalexic
We get all slang on them
The only thing we're one in
Is this big mix-up
I don't think we fit together
We're not pieces of a puzzle
There's no solution to a cloud
Just put up Babel
Like nine-pins or pine trees
Stupidly resolute
Fecund but eclectic

There are infinite ways
And only one song?
I think not
Therefore I am not
Going to stop
Putting up Babel
In every wind
Every hurricane
Like a batch of kites
Like dykes
Like mixed market food courts
And thrice-shuffled smorgasbords
We're splitting hairs
Resisting style
Down with fashion

We don't care
We're putting up Babel

And at the top
Having stopped
At the end of atmosphere
We'll lean out
High over god and all the angels
And shout as one
A trillion words for sky

THE TEN QUESTIONS?

They were originally called the ten questions?
Thou shalt not kill?
Thou shalt not steal?
There are many question marks missing
From translations of the bible?
Man shall have dominion over the birds and the beasts?
Turn the other cheek?
Is there anything else in all typography
That looks so much like a shepherd's crook?
How could the disappearance of the question mark
Be accidental?
Why would anyone denude the bible
Of its most powerful symbol
When god himself is more of a question
Than an answer?

ALL MY FUQS (Frequently Unasked Questions)

What is the word for word?

What are the other words for thesaurus?

Would you rather keep falling
or hit bottom?

The wha? on terror

Does the arrow look back?

Who built the ark? (No-one! No-one!)

What do you call a couple
of monotheists?

When you water your soil
do you soil your water?

Does a fool answer rhetorical questions?

Why do we say it angrily —
"Enough!"

Is death the end of dying?

Where does the spin stop and the revolution begin?

COUGH LOG

Key in ignition cough you can't turn off
Stutter cough
Bubble cough caught in phlegm
Cough you have to tuck
Your lungs back in after
Scuff cough of file over nail
Sandpaper cough
Black flag flap cough
Wet cough of shale
Croak cough of the frog
Caught in the jaws of a dog
Bellows cough gallows gasp
Furnace cough
Raw rasp five foot fade out cough
Shovel scrape full in the face spatter cough
Clatter-cough coughing up matter
Hawking up data from the inner lung
Fist-splattering mad hatter cough
Ripping the lung
Belly cough that breaks a rib
Exploding cough that splits your lip
Cough like a band saw in birch bark
Scalding cough like steam from a radiator
Cough that rattles and spits — an ossuary
In a forest fire
Cough of ages cough our ancestors
Coughed in all the plagues
Coughs that scrape the lungs
Like last dishes in famine
Baby coughs
Hydra cough you can't stop
Coughs like moths beating air to red shreds

First cough of the cold that kills you
Last cough of a flu
They said would never end

RE:VERSING LOT

Lot slows, waiting
but she doesn't catch up
she must have looked back
must have disobeyed

Lot appears to freeze-frame
but not just Lot
everything stops
his two daughters stop
the fleeing carrion stop
the small escaping ravens stop
and slowly, haltingly, as Lot's will winds
his being backwards against time

everything begins to reverse its flight

When Lot gets to her he's shocked
the beloved face
crystalline

Enraged Lot draws back time
further yet
till her head turns
and the salt falls
and she resurrects

And now he's done what he's done
he's resurrected one

Reverse Lot can't stop

All the way back

through the fabled gates
of back door city
ass first Lot and his family walk

With each step another
burned infant of Sodom
rises from incineration
tattered flesh zipped up
cool to mother's touch

Everywhere burning shirts
are flung high in waves of healing

Cascades of resurrection
Roll out exponentially
from him in all directions

Pillars of fire hurtle skyward
into the arms of their maker
as Lot, the epicentre, trots
heels-first home

Sodom is saved, angels expelled
Gomorrah too is restored

God's hate crime erased

DEVIL/DOUBLE MEME SPLICE

The double is god's evil twin
God cast the double down
Jesus walked in the wilderness
And was tempted by the double
Double get behind me, he said

The double knows your weakness
The double knows your sins
The double knows where you give in
How long it takes
Beware whoever knows the double in you

Everyone has an angel on one shoulder
And a double on the other
I saw the double in a mirror
Sooner or later everyone comes face to face
With the double

FAITH/FACE MEME SPLICE

We are people of face
It is our face that makes us beautiful
America has a deep and abiding face in itself
Face is the most important thing in our lives
Our nation was built on face
Face of our fathers
Our face must be pure
We must not water down our face
We support face-based schools
We belong to face-based groups
We cater to people of face
The President is a person of great face
He has a very strong face in god
It is his face that sustains him
He has face in our men and women
In the field
Everything he does and says is
An expression of his face

NOAH'S DARK

for a long time Noah had been building
the darkness
god had told him that a great light was coming
and that when the shadows of the birds and the beasts
and the insects and the fish saw the light
they would want to go and run on savannas in it
or burst upward through the waters at it
or wriggle through light-lit soils to see the sun
and then they would be gone

so Noah built an immense dark
and he gathered the shadows of his family in it
and he gathered the shadows
of all but two of each kind of beast
all but two of the mammoths
and all but two of the aurochs
and all but two of the dodos
and all but two of the grey wolves
and all but two of the passenger pigeons
and Noah's dark grew bigger and darker
with all the herds of shadows of beasts and birds
and when the light finally came
spilling over the trees and flooding
the plains with that great all-washing dawn
Noah and all his shades
rose buoyant
above the great geysers
of luminescence
and were carried off
dark as pitch forever
beyond the cruel reach
of resurrection

REVERSE CIRCE

reverse Circe
turns swine
to men
but she always leaves
a little bit in
to remind them
where they came from
she turns the fatted calf
into a man
turns dodos into men
she morphs seal pups into
little baby men
and they multiply
reverse Circe makes
a man out of a mad dog
a famished tiger
a ravening bear
reverse Circe
turns maggots
into men
and lets them wriggle
into the men
that are meat
till they in turn
by meat are eaten
and those which were once the chickens
they are now the grocers
and those who were the calves
they are butchers now
or soldiers
or children
without mothers

or child soldiers
with no brothers
the buffalo still roam
they are the homeless
they are refugees
aliens
ever on the run
reverse Circe
pulls them all
into the whirling waters
and de-spins them

she's the transformer
she pushes thread
back onto the spindle
and there are fewer
and fewer eagles
and the sheep are all
wearing suits
and the python
is the prime minister now
and experimental rats
turned loose
are becoming psychiatrists
and vultures
are taking up gavels
and the great nations of fleas
are swarming
dying to be transformed
by the power of reverse Circe
into movie stars
population experts

diplomats

and every other
creature
in the universe
is out on the rim
circling her
unable to
avoid the spin
terrified of what's at the centre
but concentrically
ineluctably
drawn in

CAIN ENABLED

Cain tugs the knife
Quickly from Abel's guts
Seals the cut
Heals the wound
Restores his life
Hides the blade
In a sheath
Backing away from what's undone

As soon as he can
Cain removes the handle
From the blade
Draws back
All those filings he shore off
Quick and furtive
He returns the crude metal
To the rock he gouged it from
Sealing up stone and ground
It's not too late
It's not too late
Cain keeps walking backwards
Undoing his fate
Undoing even
The idea of a knife

Undoing jealousy
Undoing hate
Murder is no more
Murder is no more
Side by side
The two brothers
Finally arrive
Back at Eden's gate

FRIEND/FIEND MEME SPLICE

I owe everything to my fiends
Without my fiends I am nothing
I've had fiends all my life
My motto is
To have a fiend be a fiend
I was born to be a fiend
If you ask me what my ambition is
I'll say I want to be a true fiend to someone
Or better yet — to many
Let me never disappoint anyone who calls me fiend
My beloved is my best fiend
And I hers
For what is marriage
But a crucible for mutual fiendship
But I am also a fiend to nature
A fiend to the sky and the soils and the sea
A fiend to the sick and the weary
A fiend to those without food or clean water
I think of myself as a fiend to all humanity
And beyond that
I like to think that god is my fiend
And that one day we will all be fiends in heaven

IN BACKWARDS PHYSICS

In backwards physics
Einstein rides a beam of light
Into whatever it is
That begets light
And the clock in his left hand
Runs counter-clockwise round

But E still equals MC squared
MC squared still equals E
All equations
Must have bi-directionality
(At least)

PENELOPE

Penelope is the great heroine
Of bi-directionality
The trickster's trickstress
Fooling all those suitors with her nightly unweaving
Undoing their lives as surely as she undoes her work at the loom
And then by day
Like a fate needle caught skipping in its groove
She must weave again that same scene
She must do and undo
Day after day
Forward and reverse
Diverting them
Delaying them
Till the cursed one
The back and forth man
Odysseus the wily
Completes his complementary
Circuit or orbit
And pulls in a rush
From each suitor's veins
The long red threads
Of forward only
Time

EVE TO AND FRO

God said
don't call her
eve backwards

don't call her
madam adam
backwards

don't call her
mom
backwards
nor
ma'am
nor elle

nor
tit

nor
say you
boob
backwards
nor Mary Byram

be flammable but not imflammable
cleave but don't cleave

BACKWARDS EVE IS FORWARDS EVE

Backwards Eve is forwards Eve
She swings both ways
Whether Adam is backwards or forwards
She is the same

You want to slip away on the part of her that is nothing
You want to stay with the part of her that is everything
You are rent, torn and joined
That is why we say cleave unto her

In her smile you see where the ocean meets the shore
In her wrath you see the rocks and the fire that made the rocks too

But you can't have Eve without Eve
Her "yes" is forever infected with never
She needs you both ways and none

Though her surface flows with the will to obey
Her centre runs opposite

Even as she clasps her hands behind her back
And bows to Him
She is already reaching for the fruit

ABEL'S BI-DIRECTIONAL SONNET

Name's Abel, a male, base man
Oh who was it I saw, oh who?
Cain a maniac
Oozy rat in a sanitary zoo

Regard a mere mad rager
He lived as a devil, eh?
Drab as a fool, aloof as a bard
Never odd or even

Live was I ere I saw evil
Tug at a gut
Murder for a jar of red rum?
God damn! Mad dog

You know, I did little for you, for little did I know you
Revered now I live on. O did I do no evil, I wonder ever

PUTTING THE APPLE BACK

Putting the apple back in the tree
Bite by bite like certain birds who
Regurgitate for their young
Adam and Eve purge the taste
Of fruit from their tongues
From history — they kiss each other
Into one flesh and disintegrate
All the winds go roaring back to god
All the dust goes whirling back to god
The creatures of the land and sea
Beasts and birds flap ineluctably
Back through cracks in god's gaze
God magnetic drags the stars down with a last gasp
Distance buckles, time collapses
One word: logos fish fisherman net
All slip into the nothing and are perfect

Guelph Public Library

GOD IS SMALL
(a backwards paean)

God is small
Tinier than the grain of sand
In a dead man's eye
His word goes unheard
His will undone
God is weak
In starving limbs
God trembles
God is dying

Through feasting flies
God's eyes stare
At the unseeing
Uncaring sun
God is young
The weakest thing in the universe
His wrath is a twig in a blaze
His voice is sick mud
His call his command
Too weak to be uttered
Ever again

PRAYING IT FORWARD

Before I lose my self
I hope I may return
Some good
From the good I got
I hope I may give
To the giving that made me
That fed me
That healed me

Before I give up my matter
Back into the matter
I hope I do something
That matters
Something to move us along

Before I lose this ambition
Before I give up this tongue
Before the solid stuff slides away
I hope I drink
The full liquid cup of life
To love the taste of the earth
Before I give up
Lips and rain and thirst
For good
For all
Before I lose again
What can't be found
Let me find myself
Conscious in
Kindness
Aware of the air
And my beloved

With all her gifts
Let me find myself
Looking at her
Laughing with joy

ANGLE/ANGEL MEME SPLICE

God loves all the angles
He has an angle at his right hand
And an angle at his left
Radiant angles
Angles shelter us
They hold us and guide our way
They say each of us
Has our own guardian angle
A good angle and a bad angle
Angles of our finer nature
Angles of the unconscious
Mommy is with the angles now
Angle eyes
Fluttering on angle wings
I sensed the presence of an angle
In the room
I could tell
It was like my heart
Was touched by an angle

WE ARE ROWING BACK TO HERA

We are rowing back to Hera
Through all the waves of god
Of hymns of incantation
We are rowing up the waterfalls
And deep under the firmament
We are rowing back the arc

With a pop
We reach the top
We're in the old regime
Off with their heads
God save the queen

I am planting the British flag
In the past
We hereby lay claim
To all these linked
Yesterdays
The past is hereafter our domain

But I'm running out of breath
And the crew is scared to death
We get back in the arc
And quickly we age
Fastforward like
Argonauts on meth
We hurl the vessel forward
And so it is we came
Once more
To this strange lost shore

I LOVE A METAZOAN

Mitochondrial poetry
Mother-mediated matter
Multiply made and scattered
Like data in transition
In packets from node to node
Tracking the human
Diaspora
Genome by genome

And so I love a metazoan
She got her structure from bacteria
Her cells are full of manic replications
I am prone to doting on her gestures
Apparently encoded
To act this way through honeycomb
Inside honeycomb inside
Hive after hive
Of genome
In the genome
Yes I love her
Like the last Russian doll
Like the last colour at the heart of a blackball
She exudes chemicals
Catalysts, her scripts finish mine
Scratching the graffiti
Inside our skins
To hypertext
Till they connect
Mind to mind
To take us both somewhere
Inescapable
Fast

And so we are as the codes command
I am the father of a trillion typewriters
And she is the mother of all hands

MONEY/MOMMY MEME SPLICE

Just give me mommy
I work hard for my mommy
You need mommy to get by in this world
You have to save your mommy
Let your mommy grow
But don't let mommy take over your life
Don't get too attached to mommy
Mommy can weigh you down
Use your mommy wisely
Keep your mommy in a safe place
Mommy is just a tool
Mommy is a symbolic system
We are in a mommy obsessed culture
Mommy hounds
Slaves to mommy
We spend our whole lives scrabbling for mommy mommy mommy
Filthy mommy, blood mommy
Hypnotized by the power of mommy
We are all in the pocket of big mommy
Good mommy bad mommy
What is this insane lust for mommy
Mommy is being driven down devalued
We have not been very smart about our mommy
When interest rates are low mommy is cheap
Mommy destroys human relationships
Just throw mommy at it
Mommy changes everything
I have no mommy-sense
I'm bad with mommy
Mommy burns a hole in my pocket
I have to go begging for mommy in the streets
I hate mommy

I reject mommy
Mommy is the root of all evil
But it is so hard to live without mommy
I'm trying to hold on to my mommy
But everybody wants my mommy

What happened to our mommy?
We took huge risks with our mommy
And we lost
We are completely broke
We totally wasted our mommy

BUCKET LIST

use a fish
to catch a hook

bring the canon
with the cannon

give generously
to the oppressor

reduce use of the juice!

turn loose the dogs of poetry
on the murderers of language

hang a million
mass murderers
at once

get everything
from nothing

AUTHORITY IN REVERSE

Authority in reverse
Where is it?

What? Everything
Is a question?

The polar opposite
Of moral?

The six
Black dot eyes

Probing at probability
With backwards dice?

It has been determined
They will wind up in your palm?

Authority in reverse
Disobedience to obsession?

You're a gambler
In a completely predictable universe?

CHICKEN PHYSICS FROM SCRATCH

the only absolute
is the speed of a chicken
you can never know for sure
where a chicken is
when the light from a chicken
reaches you it is already billions of years old
nothing can move faster
than a chicken
a chicken is uncertainty itself
a chicken is a function
of the egg
light cannot escape from
a collapsed chicken
information cannot die
even in a collapsed chicken
a chicken is a trance-mission
the chicken is trans-chicken
in mid broadcast
all chickens are media
getting static
you can tune a chicken in
but you can't tune a chicken out
a chicken is a message
we miss
we don't get chicken
we forget to get chicken
chicken is a squawking amnesia
when you see wings in plastic
you are looking
at dead memory
a chicken is a web
of recollection

chickens count you
before you hatch
they scratch their
chicken math
assessing future
excess
a chicken is
a calculator
with a beak
trying to peck
the eye out of the earth
whenever two chickens connect
they are joined forever
chickens are the things
we don't say
I hear the rabble
of chickens over all else
you can't turn one chicken
into another
there is no way
to properly value
even one chicken
a chicken is pure context
it is a poetry machine overwound
once the sun gets in a chicken
it can't get out
chickens are the sound
of life after death
there are no atheists
in the chicken coop
the rooster's call
is the sound of pure immorality

a chicken is an itch
made bird
they are innumerate
mathematicians
tasty wizards
they are obsessive assessors
keeping accounts in the dust
but they themselves
are unassessable
you can't count chickens
even after they hatch
and when they die
there is nothing in the world
louder than one chicken

WAVING TO A PHOTON

Waving to a photon
Slow-mo in oceans
Of evidence
Floating away on a glance

I've got perspective issues
With the fringe stuff
It's crowding my corners
Brimming the rim
With fluffy complexities

What! What! What!
I set up a stutter
To do it automatic
Waving to the photons
Every single one
Like the queen
On coronation day
Like a traveller
In a passing train
What! What! What!
To a windmill in the rain
To every drop

Bye — bye — bye
My heart made of particles
My thought made of patterns
My mind entropic, steamy
A mess of what, what, what
In the flotsam
Seeing, not seeing
Seeing not, seeing

Switching the photons
On and off
Waving to the wave
The wave waving back
Wondering what? What? What
Do I become
Now that I've been seen

And what not?

OUR CHILDREN ARE EXPLOSIVE

Our children are explosive
They blow up at anything

They sit in their rooms and
Smoulder

New born babies particularly
Have such short fuses

They are so full of rage
Megatons of descendants

Having meltdowns in market places
Going ballistic in schools and museums

We drop our children
Indiscriminately on innocent civilians

They set off other children in chain reactions
They have no limits

They take soul-numbing drugs
And erupt in line beside you

You have to tiptoe
Around them

Our children are so triggered
So high strung

They are supersensitive
Like landmines

Just waiting to be stepped on

When they look at me
Their eyes are more like bullets
Than bullets themselves

They are famines
Waiting to happen

SKATER SON

He makes a roller coaster of a handrail
Rides the revolutions

Lateral and long
The boy is surfing a stone curve

Almost sideways
Skating street and step alike

Loose on architecture
He winds and sways his way

To and from school
Or just down the road a piece

And back balanced on a leaf
Sailing the stairs

Taking back all the rivers
That were ever taken

Making the rivers be
Everywhere

THE EARTH IS ALREADY DAMMED

O why are the salmon runs ruined
And the mighty deltas parched and dry

Because the earth is already dammed

Why is the Amu Darya withered
And the wetlands shrunk to sterile salt flats

Because this earth is constantly dammed

Why do the Sandhill cranes tremble
On their long legs
Landing nowhere after nowhere
In diminishing migrations
Why do those liquid slaves the rivers
Stand still in their chains
Stripped of their old ways
Never to spill free again upon the land

Because the whole earth is repeatedly dammed

Dammed for power
Dammed just to make work

Every river across the globe
Locked, blocked toxic

It is time to stop
The constant damming of the earth

Free the great currents, unleash
The torrents of the Nile on a thousand miles of thirst

Let the whorling eddies of the held back Platte
Revivify the wetlands

Re-circulate the stacked sediments
Bring back the hatcheries

The green thatch of cottonwood
Upon arid banks

I want to hear the rush and hush
Of free green water

Restored to ancient circuits
I want to see the earth de-cursed

Its rivers resurrected
The damages reversed

I want a free-flowing re-blessed world
I want people to stop damming this planet

WMD II

We must dream
We must demonstrate
We must defy
With mass disgust
With more diplomacy
We'll meet directly
We'll make deals
We'll make demands
Way more discussion
Way more definition
Way more deliberation
We must do
What mercy demands
War must desist
Who makes decisions?
We make decisions

SCRATCH THE SKY

Scratch the sky
Turntable son
One groove
Against another
Blue backwards
Against the indigo that was
What a shade to loop!

You play the grain
Against the grain
Re-art the artefacts
But in reverse
Spinning time against time
One vandal move
After another
Sometimes singing
Sometimes beat-boxing
Over the groove

Turntable son
Reverse the shine
Against the sun
Rub the song back
Into forwards time
Play the itch against itself
Scratch at rings of mind
When they want to run
Into themselves
And out
Raw/new
Fingerprints
Reversed and spun

Into their own whorls
As they push back against
The way of this world

PLAYING THE BEATLES BACKWARDS

sometimes the beatles
broke yoko ono up

she said so
she said she loved

the way they made
her laugh

MY HANDS SPLINTER ON

My hands splinter on
More branch lightning
From the long list
Of lightning hands
That struck in anger
Exponential fingers
Gripped in one fist
Full and hard
I smacked him in the head
My own son!

My hand my hand
That went through a machine
Crushed flat
My hand I got
From killers of kings
My hand that branched down out
Of time at me with a mighty clout
Of blood
I struck my eldest
In the head
Full-fisted hard
His head sideways
On the ground
I confess
I confess

That's the worst thing
I've ever done

HEADACHE DIARY

The slow stunning cotton batten one
Stuffing the veins, crammed behind the eyes
The occipital black bruise
Clotted into ribbons at the base of the skull
Nailed through the nose
The grape in a vice
Bulb against nerve one zigzagging
The vision, cracking the orb
Blood bag ballooning in the brain stem
Puking visionary light-streaked headache
That tastes of intestine
That tastes of the grave
Cold cadaver headache
That 3 Advil won't stop
Slow creeping three day
Smog spot
Widening in the grey stuff
Like a wet wing of blood
Shattering skull and skin alike
Jigsaw face headache in puking pieces
Down on your knees
To the god in the bottom
Of the bowl
Headache
Like a broken bell
In full toll
Headache
Like a broken bell
In full toll

BOMB/BALM MEME SPLICE

I

The blue balm
Slips in somehow
Under our radar
Flies among us
She's the balm
She's the balm for everyone
No matter what your complaint or ailment
She's the balm
The balm for the broken hearted
And the balm for fractures
She's the balm for diphtheria
And for the ache of loss
She's the balm for
The wicked and the good
A wave of healing follows
The invisible flight of the blue balm
As she goes
Among skyscrapers
And mud huts
The drug companies are after her
She has no licence
She has an illegal indica propeller
The blue balm
With her miracle palms
Healing and making whole
Bringing ease to pain
And cool to burning
A sudden touch of soothing calm
And then she's gone
The blue balm
Ever on the run

II

We hope and we pray
That our sons and daughters
Will grow up to be balmers one day
We need more balmers in Gilead
We must put up pictures of balmers in the schools
And call them heroes
We must raise a generation of balmers world-wide
There still are not enough balmers
Or balms
We need to make bigger and better balms
And apply them liberally
Let us bring our hands down
All around the earth and soothe us
The world is a raw ragged burning skin
And all humanity longs for the balm

NOT A MOSAIC

Not a mosaic
But ten tin cans tied
To the same tail

Not a mosaic
But a multiple outcome puzzle
Capable of making strange
Other Canadas

We're collaging
We quilt
We speak everything
And eat widely
Not a mosaic
But a smorgasbord

A clutch of magnets
Mutually repelled

10 dominoes
Each letting the other stand

Not home and native land
But native lands, native countries

Not just law
But justice

Not just a future
But a history

WORD/BIRD MEME SPLICE

All too soon the words migrate
They spend the winter elsewhere
We see them going and we are silent

In spring listen to our chatter as the words return
The air, the trees, the skyscrapers
Are full of words on wing

The word has a nest where it lays its eggs
And soon the little word-eggs arrive
Words are hatching
Words are catching
Words are singing in the trees

Hey wordie, hey hey little wordie
Where'd you get dem wings?

In children's drawings there are always words in the sky
Spread like softened Ws

Because all words are questions
They fly in flocks to make sense of the sky
Because god sees the little word falling

One day we will run screaming from words
That want to peck us to death
They will crash through our windows
Loud words in a cloud of shrieks ever thicker

Why would you put a word in a cage?
Why would you want a word swinging on a little perch?
Saying itself over and over: word word word word

POETRY HAS NOT

poetry has not pushed back autumn
its words were whipped away like so many leaves

the government has not been able to stop it
the trees are nearly bare

people with rakes scrape the back of the earth
beneath gaunt wooden skeletons

the wind seeping in like water
and hanging there damp

the sun can hardly get through
it's drunk, it's faint, its day is done

all those who insist that time must move forwards
have won

RAIN, TRUST ME

Rain, trust me
Is more than mere information

But it is not quite
Knowledge

Yet

There is an old saying —
There is no wisdom

In what doesn't
Get wet

MIXAMS AND PREVERBS
[Sayings For a Party Game]

there is no blasphemy
like religion itself

lies don't tell themselves

everything obscures everything else

wickedness loves stupidity

the worst evil
is evil yet to do

one lash
starts the herd

never leave them
wanting less

you can always tell
the same joke twice

look big
and carry a little tazer

no amount of travel
will get you to the other

the medium is the large

variable is the new
changeless

evil is consciousness

only conscienceness is consciousness

the last thing I need
is an ending

the wor(l)d is lost
in transmission

there is only one monotheism

there were three monotheists on a plane
a monotheist a monotheist and a monotheist

you can't step into the same monotheist twice

many gods
one monotheism

under the monotheistic sky
chaos of birds

one wind
many scarecrows

one blasphemy
many religions

each link blames the others
for the chain

the shovel blames the heel
for the grave

the harp won't sing
if it's not plucked

you can't bring the well to the cup

there are no shadows
in the sun

O ye of little doubt

the wave moves on
without the water

the wave moves on
without the hand

don't miss your bliss

god exists only in kindness

the will to do good
versus
the will to do well

to do good
and well at the same time

freedom is having nothing
and giving everything

you can't do it all
and nothing

you can't do good
with evil

you never know where
a good thing is gonna come from

deity is theory
with personality

glamour is a
face-based religion

a pig has no word
for sausage

if you pull one sausage
you pull the whole string

there is no time for immortality

there is no time...
only suspense

infinity did not allow for specifics

even the good can be ruined by love

confession hounds the liar

the inscrutable obvious

oil is the opiate of the masses

the land of plenty
(of weapons of mass destruction)

evil could do nothing without the good

life liberty and the pursuit of
weapons of mass destruction

I'll save your life if you'll save mine

the boy who cried
weapons of mass destruction

his soup is bigger than his pot

masses of weapon destruction

curiosity killed the catastrophe

it takes love to make love

please do not stare at the observers

IMMEDIATE IS TOO SOON

Immediate is too soon
The present keeps coming at you

Like the down escalator
When you're heading higher

The now rushes at you
Like sun trying to get out of a fire hose

You have to swim so fast
Just to stay still

Place won't anchor you
Its carpet keeps getting pulled out

And the moment rushes in
Pushing your raft further and further off

We say wait a moment
But a moment is a hurricane

A deluge of presence
Like water when the levees break

It is everything happening
All at once

TRANSPORT

Nothing between me and the divine
Except what I want
What I expect
The only presence is mine
And even that
Mediated by intellect

There is nothing up against the nerves
No filter, we are raw, but we are not essence
We are transport

There's a slight delay in presence
The present is pre-sent
No two events can happen at once

You are everything between sender
And receiver
But you aren't the message

You begin after the question
And end before the answer

WE MADE EACH OTHER UP

There was no us
Nothing to want us

So we made each other up
We took two deep breaths

And imagined
We invented our creators

At the moment of making us
We made each other up

Out of sheer lust
Out of clear need

For a miracle
We invented us

Right on the spot
Where one

Cannot exist
Without the other

EVENT

Time proceeds
For each being
Event by event

Events per day
Events per year

When one event is over
A new one can begin

But sometimes in one event
Infinite other events intersect

And resolve at once

At that moment
A miracle can happen

There is only one requirement
Presence

LOVE IS BIGGER THAN ME

love is bigger than me
I can't keep it inside
it swells over my lips
streams from my eyes
it is too big for any one man
there is too much love
for one person alone to contain
even a threesome
would not be enough
love is bigger than a whole choir singing
you can't keep it in one church
love spills out
over the land
the air, the birds
cannot contain it
there is love in the world
bigger than the world
cracked open
in a billion places
by love's breathing
people must enlarge their lives
must widen their hearts
love is stretching the sky
heaven cannot hold it
how can I keep it in
I am bursting
I just have to say it
I love
I love

THE INFINITE IS CLOSING IN ON US

The infinite is closing in on us
It was once infinitely infinite
Each possible piece of it capable of containing
Infinite other infinitely infinite infinities
Endlessly endless
Anyone could take away an infinity
From some infinity
And still leave that infinity
Utterly infinite in all its original infinitude
Nothing missing
And meanwhile the infinity that is taken
Is likewise infinitely infinite in every way

And so the local is not accurately locatable
People never really are anywhere
It is impossible to put a foot down on a place
Every place is places
With infinite other places
In it, of it, from it
We can never step into the same river
Even once
There are a thousand rivers
Before our sole touches bottom
We meet a woman and think we've
Met one person
But there are infinite consciousnesses
In those eyes
A trillion smiles ignite
In that glimmer

If you slow us down
Like film you'll see there are spaces

Where we are still in time
And spaces where we are gone
And in those gone spaces, infinite other gone spaces wait

You can take time away from eternity forever
And there is still time streaming endlessly
There are eternities between
The kiss and the mouth
Tongue and pomegranate
Just as seeds will become seeds
In exponential ever-expanding pulses
We come from us
And when we come
We become and cease
And become again
Strobe-like
Dying and bursting
Delimiting the dark about us
With the charge of presence
After presence
Extremely local
But unlocatable
Hazy not just in the bed of the one
But in all the possible beds
The bed of one can become

THE SAIL CANNOT

The sail cannot deny
The wind
How can I deny
My love

You move me
You send me
I have crossed barriers
I never dreamed
With you behind me

The mirror cannot deny
The sun
All that light people see
Reflected in me
Comes from you
Because I do not look away

Can a string opt out of
A chord?
How could I be alone?
A single finger
Plucks my heart

Only to make me part
Of an arpeggio

NEW WORDS FOR NEOLOGISM

molehill mountaineers

mass martyrers

capitotalitarianism

atheist-based groups

liberterrorism

terrortorial

the beginning of a whole new error

immurderate language

murderage

civilification

the child of all battles

the wolf in shepherd's clothing

backwards Christian soldiers

anal sects

homophobaphobia

society for the advancement
of the oppressor

schismism

the panzer of think tanks

collective unconscience

the news about your neck

attention surfeit disorder

anaesth-ethics

trance-humanity

the no-fair state

it's hard out here for
the oppressor

mutu-actuality

interconnected nest

text-knowledgy

entertazerment

edutazers

libertazers

banksters

stupisfaction

the nymphomation

the skinfo

tazer-gasm

the outformation age

monotheoryism

polytheoryism

atheoryism

theoryocracy

a theoryocrat

big bang monotheists

a soul/asshole

a full circle smile

WE FIND EACH OTHER

We find each other unexpectedly
Or after quests
We find each other on buses
Or in airports
We grab the same luggage
We bump heads
We find each other face-to-face
In a stalled crowd
Each the obstacle of the other
In hockey games, in books
Ghosts connect
Opposing winds rush into one another
And out the other side
There's nowhere we can walk or fly
Disguise won't work
The rock, the tree
I see you in all of them
In time in timelessness we meet
There is no summer
In any possible world
Where I do not enter a room
And see you for the first time

EACH OTHER'S BEE

You have to take the first step
To get lost

The world won't just walk away
But if you stand still

The hummingbird will find you
And you will be eye to eye

With a sugar sipper
Each the other's dream

Just like you and me
We're each other's bee

All we have to do
Is be still and be seen

WHAT LAUGHS

Because they can't find it
Physicists call it dark matter

But light too can go unseen
Maybe it's light matter

And maybe I have light matter parts
Maybe that's what laughs
.Maybe that's what skips down the street

Maybe it was our light matter parts
That met before time

Maybe that's why we have that feeling
We haven't quite seen each other yet

Though I've been looking right at you
Searching for twenty-seven years

POEM IN WAITING

I make the poem wait
For her
It's all backed up
As though behind a dam

She just sits there
Her hands together
Prayer-like
Her head bent over
And into them
Protected

In ten of my seconds
One of hers passes
I breathe in and out ten times
Just as her first breath
Reverses the flow
Drawing the long air in
Beautiful and slow

It is the only thing
That can possibly happen
At this moment

FEMININE INTROS

feminine intros
to man endings
the funnel doubly
gendered
no innee without
an outee

all the rest is increment
ratio of one two another

male results
to girl actions
instead of a good grip
great traction
girl bits on boy bits
sandpaper
to sandpaper
scraping each other
off the grid
into pure template
finding out how
we're made

woman time
to man place
part heart
part kiss
one nerve
we
each
access

that's how much you
I am

mystical but only minimally —
never overwhelming the logic of it all
evolution's engine
piston and gear
we, making love
make time
make place
yes
make this home

that's how much me
you are

THE PAIN WOMAN

The pain woman
Should not have
Multiplied
But she was addicted
To the agony
Of the pain man

And so they sipped at each other
Doubling the torment
They joined their
Two tortures
The whole
Was bigger
Than the parts

Then the pain babes arrived
Pre-hurt, already traumatized
Driven like Greek heroes
To their accidents
The collisions, incisions
And rips
That would open them deeper
To the next generation
Of pain

I am arrowed in on pain girl
Sorrow has made her beautiful
She is pure agony to behold
But when I'm with her
We are out of sync with hell
For up from my feet
Comes this wholly ambivalent thrill

Yes I see her
As agony itself
But her kiss is
Anaesthesia

WHAT I DON'T KNOW

what I don't know
would fill the universe
except for one thing
I know I love you

everything I doubt
all at once
would stagger time
and blow place
out of the water
but beyond place
or time
be certain
I love you

you found soul
in arrogance
drew gentleness
from thorns
you gave everything
you owned
to the wind just for
wanting to
but stood firm
against the impossible
because the impossible
is not right

I talked you out of an education
but you taught me
you gave me children
you gave me leafy greens

you saturated every cell with olive oil
and got me going
on mangoes

my ingratitude
for too much
towers over Rhodes
it strides the moon
and disrespects infinity

but it is not utter
it can never now be complete
thanks to you
thanks to you

LIMITED

I'm limited
I can only see the future

when it's too late
and even then I deny it

till it's past
I need to prognosticate

just to cross the street
how will I cross time

to find you
without prophets

I need my seers
to see you

I need those who will name you
in order to have a word to call out

one day I'll predict
the ultimate transfixion

the criss-cross of
all chronologies in us

to be still
and in transmission

to be centred
but at the rim

at which point laughter
surprised joy

will out us
and from all quarters

outrage will glare
ha! here we are

I LOVE YOU FORWARDS

I love you forwards from here on in
I love you back to when you were nineteen
I love you sideways, spooning, walking
One hand each centring the butterfly
I love you vertically up to where we can see
Or where our kind may ever be
And down too, through the earth
Into the core and out the other side
In a loop about the rim
The swerve of my eyes
Skidding over your beauty like a fast car
Round a long slow curve on the California coastline
I love you laterally too — two rulers, two yardsticks
Measuring one another, trying to stay trim
Equal in every inch
I love you compressed like a baseball
Cracked a billion miles in reverse by one look
Back-asswards
Unidentified particles de-timing on the bliss front
I love you infinite but infinite in reverse too —
Beyond the so-called beginning
Right out the back end of any possible origin
I love you for words
I love you for songs
The two of us holding a dream between us
Centring the inkblot
Circling the unattainable
Giving symmetry something
To arrange itself around